Original title:
My Search for Purpose: A Comedy

Copyright © 2025 Creative Arts Management OÜ
All rights reserved.

Author: Alec Donovan
ISBN HARDBACK: 978-1-80566-234-1
ISBN PAPERBACK: 978-1-80566-529-8

## Mirthful Musings on the Road to Resilience

In a world where dreams go belly flop,
I trip on laughter, never stop.
With every stumble, I rearrange,
Like juggling eggs, I find it strange.

My coffee spills, the cat jumps high,
Is this the kind of life I try?
Yet in the chaos, joy breaks through,
Like a rubber chicken, it feels so true.

With each mishap, my hopes unfold,
In comic strips, my life is told.
I dance through puddles, wear mismatched socks,
Life's a circus, full of knocks.

So here I stand, a clown with glee,
Embracing the mess, just let it be.
Through humor's lens, I see the light,
In every blunder, the future's bright.

## The Irony of Intention

I set my goals like dominoes,
But every poke just makes them pose.
I planned to shine, but here I sit,
In a tangle of plans, oh what a wit.

The road to success is lined with jest,
With every fall, I question the best.
I aimed so high, but what a scene,
Like trying to bake with a spatula green.

In meetings filled with fancy charts,
I scribble jokes, I play my part.
While others fret, I laugh and grin,
Turning deadlines into carnival spins.

So here's to dreams that go awry,
In tangled paths, I still fly high.
The irony flows, as I take a bow,
For intention's a game, and I'm winning now.

## Comedy in the Chaos of Creation

In the chaos where ideas collide,
I sip my drink, with nothing to hide.
Sketching visions on napkins worn,
As my muse laughs, creativity's reborn.

With rubber bands and duct tape dreams,
I craft my world in wacky themes.
Every glitch just adds some flair,
Like a puppy's dance with slicked-back hair.

Creation's a circus, a wild parade,
Where nothing's linear, all plans fade.
I trip on my thoughts, a comedic plight,
But sketch a smile in the dark of night.

So let's embrace this zany dance,
In artsy chaos, I find romance.
With every blunder, a new surprise,
Life's just a joke wearing clever disguise.

## The Farce of Finding Fulfillment

I chased fulfillment, oh what a chase,
Through avocado toast and a fast-paced race.
But every bite was a little bland,
Like searching for treasure in a kiddie sand.

I made a list, checked it twice,
But ended up with some bad advice.
With each new trend, I lose my way,
Like trying to dance on an ice cream tray.

In the quest for bliss, I slipped on dreams,
Falling headlong into puddles of schemes.
Yet laughter echoes in every fall,
A silly riddle, after all.

So here I stand, in my wonky shoes,
Finding joy in my accidental blues.
The farce unfolds, like a slapstick show,
For fulfillment giggles, and steals the show.

## The Ramblings of a Laughing Soul

In a world of twists and turns,
I tripped on my own shoe,
I chased a dream in velvet hues,
But found a sock instead, who knew?

I pondered fate over coffee strong,
And spilled it all on my new shirt,
Laughed at the stylish clumsy song,
With patterns that made me look alert.

A rubber chicken, my trusty guide,
Tells jokes that make me snicker,
With each punchline, I take in stride,
Life's absurdity grows even thicker.

So here I dance with silly grace,
In life's strange, comedic play,
If lost, I'll just embrace the chase,
Fools remind us it's okay to sway.

## Savoring the Sweetness of the Serendipitous

Stumbling into luck's embrace,
I tripped on fortune's treat,
A jelly bean upon my face,
I licked my lips, what a sweet greet!

I found a dollar in my jeans,
Thought it must be destiny,
But it's just loose change and seems,
To vanish like my sanity.

Sipped lemonade that turned to jam,
And thought, why not make toast?
With every bite, I felt like glam,
Until crumbs became my ghost.

In life's buffet, I snack with cheer,
On every mishap, every whim,
Laughter's flavor, always near,
Savoring each delight with a grin.

## Tickle Tramps on Trails of Thought

On meandering paths of whimsy's quest,
I found a feather, it tickled my brain,
Chasing ideas, quicker than a jest,
In a tumble of words, I can't refrain.

Why did the chicken cross the street?
To dodge my thoughts, oh clever fowl!
I laughed so hard, almost lost my seat,
While pondering why I wear this scowl.

A squirrel in a hat, so dapper and neat,
Offered me lessons on how to be bold,
Convinced I should venture, dance on my feet,
While singing old songs that we both know by gold.

So join me, friends, let's trip and slide,
With giggles echoing through the park,
In ticklish trails where fun reside,
Let our laughter ignite a spark.

## Revelations from a Fool's Perspective

In a moment of sheer delight,
I stared at my soup, it grinned back,
Thoughts emerged from the bubbling bright,
A philosopher in a noodle pack.

Why so serious? Said my old shoe,
As I pondered life's perplexing game,
It squeaked and laughed with a friendship true,
Binding us both in our shared shame.

I slipped on banana peels of fate,
Yet down I went, embraced the earth,
In laughter's ease, fear starts to abate,
Finding joy in each ludicrous mirth.

So here I wallow, a jester's grin,
Collecting blunders like shiny stones,
In folly's arms, I always win,
For joy is found even in tones.

## **Jokes on the Journey of Intent**

Why's the compass spinning round?
It can't find any ground!
Maps are for those who know,
But I'm lost in quite the show.

I asked a sign to point the way,
It winked and went on play.
I stumbled into a koala's tree,
And I thought it smiled at me!

My GPS has left the chat,
It's asking where I'm at.
Pizza's more direct than fate,
And I can't even get a date.

So here I roam, no route in sight,
Each misstep feels so right.
With laughter as my guiding star,
I trip, I joke, and raise the bar!

## Sarcasm Skimming the Surface of Serendipity

I sought the wisdom of a sage,
He laughed and turned a page.
"Life's a sitcom, can't you see?"
"Pick any line, just be free!"

With every twist, I learned to jest,
While fate treated me as a guest.
Doors swung wide, then slammed tight,
I chuckled through each silly plight.

A fortune cookie cracked its shell,
"You'll do great—just don't dwell!"
I nodded wisely, winked with glee,
As if it meant something to me.

Oh, serendipity, you sly fox!
Clothes mismatched, mismatched socks.
I'll dance with you in mismatched shoes,
Finding joy in the absurdity I choose!

## **Laughing at Life's Little Lessons**

If wisdom fell from trees so high,
I'd catch it like a pie!
But it lands with a heavy thud,
And I just end up in the mud.

I tried to skate on frozen lakes,
But learned about those funny breaks.
Every tumble taught me flair,
Like a clown without a care.

Chasing dreams like they're a hare,
Seems all they do is stare.
An awkward dance, here I stand,
With life's lessons unplanned.

So bring on more of these goofs,
I'll wear my smile like a proof!
For every slip and silly mess,
I laugh 'til I can't confess!

## The Playful Paradox of Passion Pursuits

What's a passion if it feels like chores?
I might as well clean the bathroom floors!
I chase my dreams with this big grin,
Then realize I forgot to begin.

With every hobby, I start to juggle,
Until it spirals into a struggle.
A painter's brush becomes a broom,
Macrame turns into gloom!

Sign me up for joy, they said,
But I tripped on the first thread!
Frolicking in the fields of wants,
Only to face the daunting haunts.

Yet through the mess, I find the fun,
In every laughter, I have won.
For passion's just the circus clown,
And I'm laughing while I fall down!

## Amusing Antics on the Search for Significance

In a crowd of wise folks, I took a peek,
Found a philosopher biting a cheek.
He scribbled on napkins, made quite a mess,
I wondered aloud, was it wisdom or stress?

A cat in a hat said, 'Join my parade!'
With chickens and frogs, I felt quite betrayed.
They danced and they twirled, oh what a sight,
And I laughed so hard, I lost track of light.

I tried to find answers in fortune cookies,
But they only suggested I join a book club.
With misfits and dreamers, we laughed till we cried,
And forgot about purpose, at least that we tried.

So here I am, still lost in the fray,
Chasing my tail like a dog in play.
But what's worth more, the laughter or find?
I'll take the giggles, they're perfectly kind.

## Jesting Along the Journey to Joy.

They said joy was found on a path that was clear,
So I took a left turn and stumbled on beer.
A sign said, 'Drink up, and forget your woes!',
So I filled up my cup, naught cared for my clothes.

A jester approached me, with bells on his shoes,
Told silly tales, and I couldn't refuse.
He juggled my worries, tossed doubts in the air,
And I laughed so hard, I forgot how to care.

We plotted a scheme for the meaning of life,
With rubber duckies and an inflatable wife.
Our genius was shining, so bright like a star,
But all we achieved was a game of guitar.

I danced through the night on this bizarre fest,
Turns out, in laughter, I find all the rest.
And perhaps, dear friend, the quest has been fun,
From jest to jest, joy's the best thing I've won.

## Whimsical Wanderings of an Aimless Soul

A compass was gifted, but I'd lost my way,
I ended up swimming where mermaids do play.
They told me my purpose was deep in the sea,
I got stung by a jellyfish, laughing with glee.

I rode on a turtle, both slow and perplexed,
Told him my troubles, he simply texted.
He said, 'Look at clouds, they drift and they sway,
Maybe the aimless just dance when they play.'

With each silly thought, I began to contend,
That meaning's a circle, it all just transcends.
The more that I wander, the more that I roam,
Every giggle I gather, I bring back home.

So if you are lost, don't fret, take a bow,
Join the ridiculous, just live for the now.
In whimsy and folly, true purpose unfolds,
In laughter and joy, embrace your wild goals.

## The Laughing Quest for Meaning


I donned a rich robe and climbed a tall peak,
To find if enlightenment's all it claims to be.
A wise old turtle just chuckled and winked,
Said, 'Breathe in the jokes, and you'll never be blinked.'

With every misstep on this mountain of mirth,
I pondered if laughter was life's greatest worth.
From pratfalls to puns, I kept falling down,
Yet the colder the air, the warmer the crown.

I tripped on a rock, fell into a pit,
Where ducks told me tales of not giving a whit.
They quacked about meaning being a big jest,
In the midst of the chaos, I felt truly blessed.

So I'm left with my laughter, my goals on parade,
The quest for a purpose is only charade.
With giggles and grins, I continue to veer,
In the heart of the frivolous, meaning is clear.

## The Jester's Guide to Finding Fulfillment

In a land of rubber chickens, I roam,
Searching for a throne made of foam.
With every slip on a banana peel,
I ponder the purpose of my next meal.

Juggling dreams like a pro in the park,
Every stumble ignites a new spark.
The laughter of onlookers fills the air,
As I trip over life without a care.

Oh, the wisdom of clowns is no jest,
In chaos and antics, we find our quest.
Each pratfall and quip leads the way,
To a joy that is found in the silliest play.

So here I stand, with pie in my face,
Embracing the chaos with style and grace.
With each silly act, I find my delight,
In this circus of life, everything feels right.

## Tumbling Through the Trials of Existence

I tumbled down a hill of socks,
Wishing for a clock that just stops.
Between the laundry and the spilt drink,
Life's a giant joke; don't you think?

With mismatched shoes and a hat askew,
I navigate life, unsure what's true.
Every wrong turn a new gag reveal,
In this circus of chaos, nothing's ideal.

I dance with the shadows of my own fears,
While tripping over hope buried in cheers.
Why so serious? I laugh till I ache,
Laughter's the best, even if it's fake.

So, I chase my dreams on a pogo stick,
With every bounce, I find my own trick.
In this slapstick journey, I'll find my grace,
Life's just a game in a silly race.

## Chuckles Amidst the Cosmic Chaos

In the galaxy of socks and cereal spills,
A comet of laughter streams down the hills.
I float on a cloud of whipped cream delight,
While aliens giggle at my poor flight.

With each star I chase, I trip on a path,
And every misstep earns a cosmic laugh.
I juggle galaxies in neon glow,
As the universe grins at my cosmic show.

Asteroids dance, and planets play too,
In this absurdity, I find my crew.
We toast with moons and laugh at the sun,
In the chaos of space, we've all just begun.

So come join the fun, leave worries on Earth,
In this comedy of life, we find our worth.
With chuckles and smiles, we boldly roam,
The universe welcomes us all home.

## The Absurdity of Aspirations

With dreams made of jelly and hopes sewn in thread,
I scribble my plans in the crumbs of my bread.
Wishing to fly but stapled to ground,
In this wacky pursuit, I'm utterly bound.

Chasing down rainbows with slippers askew,
I dance in the puddles, and sing just for you.
Every failed attempt, a new punchline appears,
My aspirations serve giggles, not fears.

I planted my dreams in the yard of despair,
Watered with laughter and sunlight to spare.
Though they grow wild, no order in sight,
In their tangled mess, my heart feels so light.

So here's to the jesters with grand aims in life,
Twisting and turning, avoiding the strife.
In the tale of aspirations, here's what I learned:
Laughter's the flame for which we all yearned.

## Chortling Through the Labyrinth of Life

In a maze of socks and old receipts,
I wander lost, dodging my own feet.
The GPS says, 'Recalculate!'
But I just laugh, it's kind of great.

With every turn, a wild surprise,
Like chasing squirrels with my own eyes.
A fork in the path leads to a cat,
Who meows, 'You're funny—just like that!'

I trip on life and start to scoff,
Like an unruly clown, I fall and cough.
A jester's grin is where it's at,
So I'll tip my hat to all of that!

Through twists and turns of life's great jest,
I'll giggle on, whatever the test.
With laughter as my guiding light,
I'll waddle on, and it'll be alright.

## The Fool's Compass: Navigating with Humor

Oh, the compass spins like a whirling top,
Pointing me where I dare not hop.
With every misstep, I can't help but grin,
Finding joy in where I've been.

A map of surprises, a treasure of laughs,
Unraveling life's quirky crafts.
In a riddle wrapped in tangled yarn,
I forge ahead, with a wink and a charm.

The fool's guide is one of fun and cheer,
Where directions are only slight and unclear.
Steering through mishaps like a rollercoaster ride,
I'll dance around self-doubt, filled with pride.

With antics and giggles at every crossroad,
I'll take my time, embracing the load.
For in this game, it's laughter I seek,
A compass of smiles makes life unique.

## Finding Clarity Among the Cuckoo

Among the cuckoos, I search for gold,
But find only tales that are wildly bold.
With each tick-tock, the feathers fly,
Quirky wisdom makes me sigh.

A bird with a hat and a monocle stare,
Says, 'Seize the day, if you dare!'
I nod along to its rhythmic quirk,
Clarity wrapped in a playful smirk.

The chatter of birds, like a comedy troupe,
Sings songs of fortune in one funny loop.
And I as the audience am left in the lurch,
As I find my own joy in this odd little church.

So I welcome confusion while holding my tea,
Laughing it off, because hey, it's just me!
Among the cuckoos, I'll find my way,
In a feathered paradise where I'll stay.

## Merriment in the Muddle of Existence

In the jumble of life, I twirl like a breeze,
With mismatched socks and a playful tease.
I navigate chaos with a wink and a grin,
Celebrating the messiness that's deep within.

My puzzle pieces don't quite align,
But who needs order when you can shine?
With giggles and quirks in a jumbled parade,
I'll dance through the muddle, unafraid.

Between each laugh and every blunder,
I find my purpose plucked from under.
In the scramble of lemons, a fresh lemonade,
I'll treasure the silly, that's how I'm made.

So here's to the follies, the quirks I embrace,
In the muddle of life, I find my own space.
With each silly moment, I realize pure bliss,
It's the laughter that binds us, who could resist?

## The Haphazard Pursuit of the Ridiculous

In the quest for meaning, I tripped on my shoelace,
A philosophical tumble in the wrong sort of place.
I asked a wise penguin for advice on a whim,
He shrugged with the confidence only fish can swim.

I scribbled my dreams on a napkin one night,
Turned out to be dinner—now delicious and bright.
I pondered my future atop a tall chair,
But all I could hear were the crickets in there.

I bought a self-help book, thought it'd be profound,
It turned out to be a cookbook—I'm food-bound!
As I fry my regrets in a sizzling pan,
I laugh at the chaos of this curious plan.

So here's to the nonsense, the laughs, and the falls,
Chasing the absurdity life freely befalls.
In the haphazard dance of what fools claim is fate,
I wear my confusion like a dazzling crate.

## Laughing in the Face of the Unknown

Peeking around corners, hiding from my fright,
I chuckled at shadows that danced in the night.
With a spoon as my sword, I charged through the gloom,
Turning worries to giggles igniting the room.

A signpost of chaos stood tall by my way,
It read: 'No refunds for yesterday's play.'
I shrugged and I grinned, flipped the map upside down,
Found treasure in laughter, no need for a crown.

Questions piled up like a heap of old socks,
I sorted and tossed them like some quirky clocks.
Why chase the stars when the earth offers pies?
With a fork in my hand, I reached for the skies!

With every wrong turn, a giggle unfolds,
In the face of the unknown, adventure is gold.
I stumble and tumble, oh what a delight,
Laughing through fumbles, I'm ready to fight.

## Revelry on the Road to Revelation

Oh, the revelry bumbles down the winding track,
With a piñata of hopes in a colorful sack.
Each strike at the truth sends confetti of doubt,
But laughing out loud is what life's all about!

I danced with my questions like partners in crime,
Each misstep a rhythm, each stumble a rhyme.
The map of my life is a doodle, a mess,
But I twirl with laughter, refusing the stress.

Disguised as a clown, I juggle my fears,
And balloon animals represent all my tears.
With each wobbly turn on this ride of surprise,
I salute the absurdity that blooms in my eyes.

So let's revel, dear friends, on this road of delight,
With a wink and a grin through the day and the night.
For in seeking the silly, we uncover our hearts,
In the dance of absurdity, life's humor imparts.

## The Absurdity of Seeking Sunshine

With sunglasses on indoors, I searched for the light,
But tripped on a cat in the dead of the night.
A map marked with giggles led straight to a wall,
I painted my dreams in fluorescent pink squall.

I climbed every ladder that led to the sky,
Only to find—just a ceiling and fry.
With a twist and a shout, I regrouped with a flair,
For the sun wouldn't judge if I danced in the air.

I thought I could catch it with my butterfly net,
But all I caught was a dinner regret.
Still laughing, I chuckled at nature's big joke,
In the absurdity of seeking, I'm just a fine bloke.

So let's race to the sunset and paint it a grin,
With whimsy as fuel, let the journey begin.
In the chase for the simple, I'm giddy and free,
For sunshine is laughter, and laughter is me!

## A Satirical Stroll through the Golden Years

With slippers on, I roam the halls,
Chasing dreams that tumble and fall.
The grandkids giggle at my wise talk,
While I forget where I parked my walk.

Each wrinkle tells a tale untrue,
Of youthful days, me and my crew.
A dance of life, a waddle and sway,
In this golden stage, I laugh away.

The bingo games are rather absurd,
With cards they've flipped, I'm often blurred.
But every loss comes with a cheer,
And sweet memories, oh dear, oh dear!

So here I prance, a jester old,
In a world where laughter never grows cold.
With every quirk, I find my place,
In a satirical stroll, I embrace the grace.

## Giggling at the Gaps in Grand Designs

Blueprints lay scattered, quite a sight,
Where did I plan my dream home right?
Walls made of wishes, doors full of doubt,
Each room's a riddle, let's laugh it out.

The kitchen's a circus, pots in a stack,
With recipes written on the back of the snack.
The bathroom's a slide, the stairs are a maze,
I giggle at my own design craze.

With every stumble, I raise a glass,
Cheers to the past and the present, alas!
Each flaw a reason to smile and jest,
In the gap of grand plans, I find the best.

So come, take a peek, join in the fun,
This house is a comedy, all in one.
Laughter echoes where dreams might fall,
Giggling at gaps, we'll cherish it all.

## The Comical Chronicles of Uncertainty

In a world of choices, I sit and grin,
With options aplenty, where to begin?
Like a cat on a fence, I sway and spin,
   Making bold plans that rarely win.

The clock ticks loud, or is it just me?
Time's a jester, oh can't you see?
In every tick, a chance to weep,
But I'll laugh at fate, not lose my sleep.

Maps of life drawn in crayon bright,
   Each line a joke, a silly sight.
With purpose elusive, I make it a game,
Oh, the chronicles of doubt, are never the same.

So join me now on this ride of cheer,
Embrace the unknown, let's toast a beer!
In the laugh of confusion, we find our way,
In comical chronicles, let's frolic and play.

## Frolicking with Fate's Follies

With every twist and turn of fate,
I slip and slide, isn't life great?
Wit and whimsy in each little blunder,
A way to navigate life's wild thunder.

Like socks on a floor, I stumble anew,
But laughter's my guide, it pulls me through.
With fate as my partner in this silly dance,
The chaos beckons, oh what a chance!

I'm drawing my path in spaghetti line,
Lost in the sauce, oh, I feel just fine.
Each folly a spark, a joke that unfolds,
Frolicking with fate in this life bold.

So join the parade, let's trip hand in hand,
Life's a comedy, oh isn't it grand?
In each fumble and giggle, we'll find our grace,
Frolicking with fate, we'll own this space.

## Chuckles in the Wasteland of Woes

In a desert of thought, I tripped on my shoe,
Searching for wisdom, but found nothing new.
Laughter erupted at every misstep,
Life's little mishaps—a comical prep.

I said to a cactus, 'What's life all about?'
It just wiggled its needles and gave a loud shout.
So I danced with the tumbleweeds, feeling quite spry,
In the brush of confusion, I gave laughter a try.

The mirage of answers was blurry at best,
I joked with the shadows, put humor to test.
Each giggle a nugget, each laugh my own clue,
In the wasteland of woes, I found joy in the view.

# A Musical Journey of Laughter and Learning

With a whistle so silly, I set out to sing,
Learning from failures, what a grand fling!
The notes were off-key, but hey, who could tell?
Harmony's a puzzle, a comical spell.

I met a wise tortoise, strumming a tune,
He croaked out advice by the light of the moon.
Dancing on banjos, we twirled in delight,
Laughter echoed through the soft, starry night.

Missteps in rhythm, oh how they abound!
Yet joyful melodies kept spinning around.
In the symphony of chaos, I proudly declare,
Each laugh a verse added to life's grand affair.

## **Giggling in the Face of Deep Questions**

Why do birds fly? I pondered one day,
But a parrot just laughed and flew away.
The universe spun, as I scratched my head,
While pondering quirks, hilarity spread.

In the depths of my thoughts, I stumbled and fell,
Chasing profound truths, but just found a shell.
A crab with a wink seemed to know more than me,
He chuckled and danced, 'Life's funny, you see?'

With questions like shadows that linger and tease,
I giggled aloud, with the utmost of ease.
In the circus of thoughts, I learned it's okay,
To laugh at the unknown, come what may!

## The Joyful Journey Through Life's Confusion

On a road paved with giggles, I stumbled and tripped,
With maps made of laughter, my ego was flipped.
Every bump was a joke, every turn was a jive,
In the chaos of living, I felt most alive.

I asked a grand owl where wisdom was stored,
He hooted and winked—'Don't take it too bored!'
So I frolicked with fairies and danced with my fears,
Finding joy in the muddle and laughter in tears.

As I wove through confusion, I found my sweet way,
With a heart full of chuckles to brighten the gray.
Life's an absurd ride, full of twists and delight,
In the joyful journey, everything feels right.

## The Quest for Meaningful Nonsense

I wandered through the fields of thought,
In search of answers, all for naught.
Chasing shadows, I tripped and fell,
Who knew breadcrumbs could cast such a spell?

With a map that led to nowhere quick,
I asked a squirrel for a useful trick.
He chuckled, saying, 'Just dance a jig!'
And I found my purpose in a silly gig.

The more I searched, the less I found,
A circus of thoughts spun all around.
In the chaos, I stumbled on delight,
A joke so deep it took flight!

So I embraced the nonsense, had a laugh,
Each absurd moment a heartfelt gaffe.
In the end, my quest was clear,
Meaning found in joy and cheer!

## Laughter in the Labyrinth of Life

I entered the maze with a frown so deep,
The walls were tall, but the jokes ran steep.
Every turn I made, I'd slip on a pun,
Finding humor in where I'd begun.

I bumped into wisdom dressed as a clown,
It said, 'Life's too short to wear a frown!'
So I turned my woes to giggles and glee,
Dancing past confusion, wild and free.

The exits were riddled with riddles and rhyme,
Each answer I found was the silliest crime.
A banana peel slipped me up once or twice,
But laughter could heal, not just suffice.

Finally, I saw the light of day,
Emerging from nonsense in a comical way.
Life's absurdity became my best friend,
Teaching me joy that never would end!

## Whimsical Wanderings in the Mind's Maze

I tiptoed through thoughts, both silly and bold,
In search of a treasure that wasn't pure gold.
Each whimsy I chased led me round in a loop,
With a giggle from dreams that danced like a troupe.

A thought bubble popped, it said, 'Let's play!'
With unicorns juggling, brightening the gray.
I climbed on a cloud, drank tea with delight,
Spinning my worries into pure kite flight.

I met a wise owl, who wore funky shoes,
It chuckled and said, 'You can't pick and choose!'
Around every corner, a giggler would greet,
With nonsense so sweet, it was hard to beat.

At last, I found joy tucked under a rhyme,
In the merry-go-round of whimsical time.
Each twist and each turn brought laughter anew,
In this maze of nonsense, I danced in my shoe!

## Clowning Around with Destiny

On my path, I saw destiny wear a big nose,
It winked at me, saying, 'Here's how it goes!'
With juggling dreams and confetti in tow,
I laughed through the chaos, feeling the flow.

Each step was a pratfall, each turn a surprise,
With epiphanies hidden in clownish disguise.
I slipped on my future, fell flat on my face,
But popped back up, filled with joy and grace.

In the circus of life, I found my big act,
Clowning around, I was never exact.
Yet in the missteps, the laughter did ring,
Teaching me the joys that comedy brings.

So here's to the flops and the goofy mistakes,
To the joy that arises when laughter awakes.
In each silly moment, my spirit ignites,
Clowning with destiny, my heart takes its flights!

## The Puns and Ponders of a Seeking Mind

In the quest for wisdom, I tripped on a riddle,
Wearing a clown nose, oh what a fiddle!
The answers are hidden behind every laugh,
I ponder in circles, a mystical path.

With questions like jests and hopes that persist,
I danced with my thoughts while striking a twist.
If finding the truth means acting quite silly,
Then color me jester, I'm laughing quite frilly.

A fortune cookie told me to aim for the stars,
But I ended up dreaming of sit-coms and bars.
Philosophy wrapped in a punchline so bright,
Makes the search for the meaning a comedic delight.

In every faux pas hides wisdom profound,
Like tripping on love while your feet leave the ground.
So here I am, joyful, with laughter in tow,
In the midst of this quest, I'm stealing the show.

## Mirthful Misadventures through the Enigma

I tried to find meaning by seeking it out,
But all that I found was a burrito-shaped doubt.
Through mazes of humor, I zigged and I zagged,
To tickle my brain, and I laughed when I lagged.

Philosophers argue, while I jest with my cat,
We ponder the universe, both comfortable and fat.
With every grand theory dismantled with glee,
I embrace all the chaos, the cosmic decree.

Like a rubber chicken, I bounce off the walls,
Each stumble a gem, as the laughter calls.
I scribble my thoughts with a grin on my face,
In the carnival of life, I'm winning the race.

So hand me the mic and crank up the bass,
For finding the joke means I'm winning the chase.
In mirthful misadventures, I'm learning to soar,
With giggles and puns, who could ask for more?

## The Jester's Lament: A Happy Dilemma

A jester in search of a serious plight,
Stumbles on laughter, oh what a delight!
With laughter as armor, I'm ready to play,
In the comic arena where worries decay.

With riddles and quips, I juggle my fate,
And hold it up high, like a fool with a plate.
Each gag is a treasure, each pun is a clue,
In the theater of life, I act like it's true.

A life coach once told me to find inner peace,
But I'm struggling hard, so I'll settle for cheese.
Each slice is a lesson, each grin a delight,
In the circus of living, I'm always polite.

In this happy dilemma, I bask in the fun,
While chasing the shadows of things yet undone.
So here's to the laughter, the joy that we share,
For as I seek meaning, I'm floating on air!

# Frolicking in the Fields of Understanding

meander through fields where the wild thoughts grow,
I trip on the daisies, but what do I know?
For purpose is planted in each little sprout,
And giggles emerge from the seeds of doubt.

With wisdom like honey dripped onto a joke,
I dance with the bumblebees, laughter a cloak.
Each flower a story, each petal a pun,
Frolicking freely, I bask in the sun.

The grass whispers softly, what's meaning, you ask?
I reply with a chuckle: it's quite the big task!
Though answers are playful, like kittens in shoes,
I'll savor the journey, I've nothing to lose.

So let's frolic together in fields of delight,
A carnival of ideas on this breezy night.
For in searching for purpose, a jest does implore,
That laughter is golden and opens the door.

## Chortles in the Shadows of Seeking

In a world of dreams and schemes,
I stumbled upon banana peels,
Slipped right into my grand plans,
With giggles as my only heals.

Maps guiding my every step,
Lead me not to golden gates,
But to a cafe that sells soup,
And discusses life with old mates.

I asked the stars for advice,
They twinkled back with smirks,
Told me to chase my heart's delight,
Just avoid the quirkiest quirks.

With laughter as my compass bright,
I'll dance through life's absurd race,
Finding treasure in the silly,
And purpose in fun's warm embrace.

## Skits of Serendipity: A Fun Exploration

Poking around in the dark,
I tripped over a rubber duck,
Giggling it quacked like a bard,
In my quest for luck, not muck.

I joined a circus of lost socks,
They spun tales of roles unmade,
Acrobats juggling life's big dreams,
With laughter's price, no dues to be paid.

A wizard said, "It's all a bluff!"
With rabbit hats and tricks galore,
In the midst of all this fluff,
I found joy was the best encore.

So here I am, no map in hand,
Just clown shoes and a slice of pie,
In the game of life so slightly planned,
I'll chortle as I pass by.

# The Humorous Hiccups of Hope

Each morning starts with a silly yawn,
As I check if hope's still here,
Hiccups of laughter greet the dawn,
With dreams that dance and disappear.

I chased a butterfly dressed in gold,
It led me into a sandwich shop,
Where wisdom served on crusty bread,
Is washed down with fizzy pop.

Thoughts of grandeur turned into pies,
Flying high on my garlic breath,
But every fall brings a big surprise,
Mirth lives on beyond the death.

With humor as a trusty guide,
I'll twirl through every twist and bend,
Finding joy in the ridiculous ride,
And laughter that jests but won't end.

## Punchlines in the Path of Purpose

On the road of zany dreams,
I found a sign that said 'Free Fun',
Toured the lands of silly schemes,
And laughed till my heart was done.

The wise old owl that wore a hat,
Said purpose is all in the jest,
"Find the punchline in every spat,
And let giggles be your quest."

So stumbling through quirky streets,
I dodged pies and quirky pranks,
Like cartoons, life throws wild treats,
Grins, snickers, and happy thanks.

I may never find the grand design,
But with a chuckle, I will sway,
For every misstep becomes divine,
In laughter's light, I'll find my way.

## Jokes Carved in the Stones of Destiny

I set out on a quest, quite grand,
With a map that led to nowhere planned.
I tripped on clouds, fell on my face,
Yet laughter echoed, what a silly place.

The wise owl hooted a pun so bright,
Said, "Find the path, or just take flight!"
While squirrels debated the meaning of cheese,
I pondered life's riddles while dodging the bees.

The rocks were witty, the trees wore hats,
With every step, I swapped tales with cats.
The universe chuckled, I caught its grin,
In the search for meaning, the fun begins.

So here's to the journey, the laughs we share,
While the purpose hides, we'll dance by the flare.
With jokes carved deep in each twist and stone,
I found my joy, and I'm never alone.

## The Hilarious Search for the Hidden Self

In mirrors that reflected my confused face,
I searched for the self in a crowded space.
With rubber chickens and pies in hand,
I declared myself the funniest in the land.

The sages spoke riddles, wrapped in frowns,
While I ballooned my way through silly towns.
Each twist and turn, a pratfall or jest,
Each question I asked, just furthered the quest.

I wore socks that clashed with my boldest dreams,
Chasing laughter, or so it seems.
The hidden self, I sought with flair,
As I tripped over laughter, without a care.

In the end, it's not about what I find,
But the chuckles and giggles that fill up my mind.
For in every mishap, a truth takes its stand,
The search is a joke that's beautifully planned.

## Absurd Adventures in the Meaningless

On a journey through nonsense, I found a clue,
A walrus in slippers just waiting for stew.
With penguins tap dancing on marshmallow skies,
I couldn't help laughing, oh, how time flies!

The mountains wore glasses, absurd and spry,
While clouds floated by, dressed like a pie.
Each signpost I passed said, "Don't take yourself too,
Life's a circus; grab a ticket or two!"

In search of the meaning, I met a wise crab,
Who offered me jokes wrapped up in a lab.
"The secret of life? Just wear a big hat!"
I giggled aloud, and sat down to chat.

So here's to the absurd, the joy in the ride,
Who cares if the meaning has nowhere to hide?
With laughter as compass, I'll dance in the void,
In a world so ridiculous, I'll never be bored.

## Wandering Through Whims with a Smile

With a grin on my face, I ventured afar,
Wandering whims beneath the bright star.
The path was a merry-go-round, wild and bright,
Every twist and turn brought unending delight.

A jester advised me, "Just follow the fun,"
As I chased after giggles, oh what a run!
The trees told me tales, the flowers sang songs,
In this garden of laughter, it's where I belong.

I wore shoes made of pudding, a crown out of cheese,
Frolicking freely with giggling breeze.
Through puddles of joy and rivers of glee,
In this whimsical world, I just let me be.

So here's to the wander, the chuckles we find,
Each smile a treasure the universe signed.
In this playful parade, I'll carry my cheer,
For joy is the purpose that's always near.

## Puns, Puzzles, and the Pursuit of Happiness

A jester's hat upon my head,
I roam through life with joy and dread.
Each pun I crack, a riddle too,
Searching for laughs like a treasure crew.

In life's maze, I navigate,
With silly jokes that never wait.
Puzzles solved with giggles bright,
For happiness, I take a flight.

From ticklish toes to giggling tears,
I chase the fun between the fears.
With every smile, I twist the fate,
A comical dance, let's celebrate!

Through laughter's lens, the world's a game,
And joy's the prize—oh, what a claim!
So here's a jest—join in the spree,
In this pursuit, we're wild and free.

## Laughter Lines on the Tomb of Ambition

On gravestones marked with dreams unmade,
I write my jokes and never fade.
Ambition's ghost, it makes me laugh,
For dreams are but a silly gaffe.

I carve out lines in smiling stone,
A comedy of woes well-known.
With every chuckle, I dig deeper,
For laughter makes the darkness cheaper.

The tombstone jokes, they keep me light,
In spectral whispers, "What's the fright?"
So here I stand with snickers loud,
Turning ambitions into a crowd.

I raise a glass to dreams unspent,
And to the joy in every bent.
For laughter reigns where hopes may fail,
A merry heart will always sail.

## Bantering with the Universe

Under stars that wink and tease,
I share my thoughts with cosmic breeze.
The universe chuckles, oh what fun,
As I debate with every sun.

I tickle fate with playful jibes,
As chaos dances, joy subscribes.
With every twist, I take a stand,
Negotiating with the grand.

"Is destiny a cruel old fool?"
I ask amidst the cosmic pool.
With humor as my guiding star,
I twirl and whirl, it's never far.

So here's my banter with the night,
In laughter's glow, I find my light.
Though galaxies may twist and bend,
With jokes and smiles, I'll make amends.

## The Lighthearted Look at Life's Twists

Life's a rollercoaster, oh what a ride,
With loops and turns that I can't hide.
I scream and shout then burst with glee,
Each twist a chance for comedy.

Through ups and downs, I find my place,
In giggles bright, I take my grace.
For every fall, there's laughter near,
A lightened heart will persevere.

Uneven paths lead here and there,
Yet every stumble leads to flair.
I trip, I laugh, and tumble bright,
In this funny dance, I take flight.

So come along, let joy be our guide,
Through life's madcap and fun-filled ride.
With hearts aglow, we'll twist and cheer,
In this silly life, let's disappear.

## The Lighthearted Pursuit of the Unattainable

In the pursuit of what seems bright,
I tripped over my own delight.
I asked a sage, then lost my train,
He laughed and said, 'You're already insane!'

I searched the skies for answers clear,
Only to find my doubts adhere.
With every step, I sought a clue,
But tripped on thoughts of what I knew.

My coffee spilled, a sign perhaps,
Of chaos in my endless laps.
Yet friends will say, 'Just take a break!'
As laughter bubbles, it's joy we make.

So here's my quest, not grand or bold,
Just loving laughter as I grow old.
With every fumble, I find my way,
In silly moments, I choose to stay.

## Witty Wonders Along the Winding Path

Amidst the twists, I quest and roam,
With every joke, I feel at home.
A map? Oh no, too serious that,
I'd rather chase a playful cat.

With laughter as my guiding star,
I danced across the fields from afar.
Silly stones sang out my song,
Reminding me that life's not long.

I stumbled on a patch of fun,
Witty wonders, not just one!
Each giggle from a startled bird,
Reminds me joy can be absurd.

In winding ways, I find surprise,
With sharp wit and the brightest eyes.
My path may twist, but that's okay,
For laughter lights the silliest way.

## The Discovery of Joy in the Jumbled

In chaos swirled, I sought delight,
A jumbled mess, a pure delight.
Unraveled socks and missing shoes,
Make unexpected paths to choose.

Amidst the clutter, treasures found,
A rubber chicken, oh, how profound!
I tossed it high, it landed wrong,
Yet laughter came, my heart's sweet song.

Messy rooms and tangled dreams,
Exist in colors, not just schemes.
I bump my head on laughter's throne,
In jumbled joy, I find my own.

So if you're lost in life's great pile,
Embrace the chaos, wear a smile.
For joy's not clean, but wild and free,
In every mess, there's jubilee.

## Chronicles of Comedic Clarity

With quips and jests, I write my tale,
In comic strokes, I set the sail.
Each laugh a page, each giggle a line,
In clarity that feels divine.

From silly slips to absurd stunts,
Through life's great farce, I take my hunts.
The chronicles unfold with grace,
As I stumble, trip, embrace the space.

With every fumble, wisdom grows,
In comedy, the truth just glows.
I pen my blunders, bold and proud,
And find my voice among the crowd.

So raise a toast to lessons light,
In laughter's glow, the world feels right.
For through the quirk and every spree,
Comedic clarity sets me free.

## Giggles in the Gaps of Understanding

In a world so wide and strange,
I trip over thoughts that rearrange.
Seeking wisdom, I sway and spin,
Bumping my head, let the laughter begin!

Questions float like balloons in air,
Each pop a riddle, a silly dare.
Chasing shadows, I giggle and fall,
Who knew wisdom could be such a brawl?

Frogs in suits sing me a tune,
Dancing round a floppy moon.
With every slip, I find delight,
In the madness, I dance through the night!

So here's to the gaps, wide and tall,
Where laughter echoes, once and for all.
In fits of joy, I find my way,
Through the nonsense, I'll frolic and play!

## Nonsensical Musings of a Curious Mind

With a feathered cap and shoes askew,
I ponder the sky, which seems rather blue.
Is the cloud a sheep or a giant's hat?
I giggle aloud, what do you think of that?

Twirling thoughts like spaghetti strands,
I scribble riddles with whimsical hands.
What's the point of an upside-down cake?
Maybe it's just for a funny mistake!

Leaping from ideas like a frog on a spree,
I chase after dreams, oh so carefree.
The more I search, the more I find,
That nonsense is gold in the curious mind!

So let the silliness guide the way,
In the puzzling chaos, I choose to stay.
With a wink and a grin, I float like a kite,
In a world filled with whimsy, everything's right!

## The Jester's Leap into the Abyss

At the edge of reason, I take a bow,
Dancing with shadows, I'm learning how.
With a red nose, I plunge so deep,
Into the void where chuckles leap!

Juggling fears like ripe ripe fruit,
I slip on a banana, laughter is cute.
How far does the abyss have a floor?
The answer's unclear, but I want more!

A tumble, a roll, a pratfall proud,
The silence that follows, then bursts into loud.
I swim in the giggles, let them surround,
In the jester's leap, true joy can be found!

So bring on the chaos, let madness reign,
In each funny stumble, there's little pain.
With a heart full of laughter in the dark,
I dance on the edge, like a mad golden lark!

## Laughter as a Lantern in the Dark

In the nighttime fog, where shadows dwell,
I flicker my laugh, a bright, silly bell.
With snorts and chuckles, I light my way,
Each giggle a beacon, come what may!

Wandering paths of thoughts askew,
I trip on puns like a fool in a shoe.
What's this twist in the plot of the night?
Just my silly brain taking flight!

Each tickle of humor, a spark so grand,
Illuminates parts of a quirky land.
A jolly old soul mixed with whimsy bright,
Shining through laughter, chasing the fright!

So let's share a chuckle, a jest or two,
In the darkness, it's all that we can do.
With laughter as lantern, we'll dance on this quest,
In the comedy of life, we're truly blessed!

## **The Joyful Confusions of a Questing Heart**

In a world of signs and glaring lights,
I tripped on dreams and silly flights.
Chasing rainbows that led me here,
I laughed at clouds like they were near.

With maps that twisted and roads that bent,
Every wrong turn was a merry event.
A compass that spun like a yo-yo fast,
Pointing to nowhere — what a blast!

I asked the stars for a guiding clue,
They winked and said, 'We're lost too, boo!'
Tickled by questions that danced in my mind,
The answers I sought were nowhere to find.

So here I wander with glee in my chest,
Joyfully lost, I'm feeling so blessed.
For in this chaos, I find my cheer,
Life is a joke, and laughter's the beer!

## A Chuckling Odyssey through the Uncertain

Set sail on a ship made of outgrown dreams,
With an engine powered by giggles and gleams.
The horizon's a riddle with no perfect clue,
Yet I steer through mishaps, oh yes, it's true!

I met a seagull who claimed to know fate,
He squawked out riddles that made me relate.
In storms of confusion, I danced on the deck,
Waving at clouds while avoiding the wreck.

With treasure maps drawn in crayon and cheer,
I discovered that laughter is the best souvenir.
From pirates of paradox to mermaids of jest,
Every misstep is just part of the quest.

So here I remain with my grin and my zany,
Finding joy in the wacky, all bright and grainy.
This odyssey glows in the light of the sun,
Embracing the wild as I frolic and run!

## Amusing Myths on the Road to Realization

Once upon a road, paved with whimsy and jest,
I met a wise turtle who said, 'Take your rest!'
He offered me cookies and tales of delight,
While squirrels debated the meaning of night.

A fox with a top hat claimed to be sage,
He spoke in riddles, I laughed at the stage.
With every tall tale, the truth took a swim,
And myths led the way on a delightfully dim.

I learned from a snail who moved at his pace,
That purpose is often a curious chase.
With each joke and laughter, I grew ever bold,
In the midst of uncertainty, adventures unfold.

So I dance on this path, barefoot and free,
Collecting the stories like leaves from a tree.
As the legends unravel, hidden gems play,
Life's a grand jest, in a quirky ballet!

# Fables of a Fool and His Folly

In a village quite odd, where ducks wore bright hats,
Lived a fool with a heart and a taste for chitchats.
He searched for his fable with zeal, not a care,
While singing love songs to the wind in his hair.

He sought wisdom from trees that giggled and swayed,
But branches just whispered, 'You misheard what we said!'
With every tall tale spun from whimsy and cheer,
His folly turned laughter into something quite dear.

He juggled his dreams like ripe, juicy fruits,
While telling the bees his confounding pursuits.
In dance with the daisies, he'd twirl and he'd spin,
Proclaiming to all that the joy's found within!

For every mistake birthed a chuckle anew,
The fool learned that folly's a part of the brew.
So here's to the quest, be it silly or grand,
In the laughter of life, we all understand!

## Sips of Serenity from a Cup of Jokes

I sip my coffee, chuckles rise,
The barista's puns are quite a surprise.
With every slurp, another jest,
Who knew caffeine could be such a fest?

Each giggle grounds me, that's for sure,
Life's absurdities, I gladly procure.
Lost in laughter, I find my way,
A clumsy dance in the light of day.

I drop my spoon, it clinks and rolls,
A symphony of not-so-great goals.
But with each spill and every blunder,
I laugh until I'm lost in wonder.

So here I sit with a grin so wide,
Life's little jests are my joyride.
Each sip takes me a step more near,
To find the meaning behind each cheer.

## A Satirical Sojourn Through Life's Maze

In a maze of shoes, I search for my size,
A quest for wisdom, and oh, what a prize!
Corners of chaos and paths of delight,
Why is it that wrong turns feel so right?

I ask a squirrel for some sage advice,
He shrugs and munches on a nut that's nice.
My compass spins in a befuddled dance,
Should I listen to fate or take a chance?

With every twist, there's humor unfurled,
As I trip on my dreams, they tumble and swirl.
Each folly a step toward blissful absurd,
I'll take the ridiculous over what's blurred.

So I wander, I ponder, I giggle away,
In this maze of life on a whimsical day.
With folly as guide, I'll conquer each phase,
Laughing my way through this comical haze.

## Fumbling Toward Enlightenment with a Grin

I tripped on a thought, it had legs like a cat,
Chasing enlightenment, I looked like a brat.
With each little fumble, I chuckled aloud,
Why is wisdom never couched in a crowd?

I climbed a tall mountain to find the right view,
Lost my footing, and fell, as I always do.
But laughter erupts when I land on my face,
Maybe humility's part of this race.

I met a wise sage who spoke in a rhyme,
His words flew away, a real waste of time.
With my notebook empty, and no pearls to note,
I sketched funny doodles, my creative quote.

So here's to the stumbles that lead us to glee,
Each pratfall a step in this folly of me.
With a grin on my face, I continue to roam,
Fumbling through life, I've made it my home.

# Musings in the Key of Comedy

In a piano bar with a clunky key,
I played my thoughts, out they flew just like me.
The notes were absurd, yet they danced and swayed,
With humor as rhythm, my worries just frayed.

I juggled my dreams like a clown with flair,
Dropping the silly ones without a care.
Each misplaced hope a laugh track in disguise,
I find joy in chaos; it's such a surprise!

In the theater of life, I'm a lead in a farce,
With pratfalls and antics, I embrace every spars.
The audience chuckles, I bow with a grin,
Finding purpose in laughter, oh, where to begin?

So let's tap our feet to the beat of the jest,
In the key of comedy, we're all truly blessed.
With each note I play, I unveil my bright side,
In this symphony of life, come take a ride!

# A Comedy of Errors and Epiphanies

In a quest for grand design,
I tripped over my own shoe.
Maps made of spaghetti strands,
I thought I found the clue.

Chasing dreams in silly hats,
Only to find a cat.
The guidebook had jokes inside,
That I could barely spat.

I stumbled through the fields of thought,
With a rubber chicken keen.
Each signpost offered hints and laughs,
A twist in every scene.

But in laughter's light embrace,
I found a hidden place.
Lost within the merry maze,
Where joy leads to my grace.

## Laughter Echoing in Search of Substance

I marched with socks that didn't match,
A symbol of my plight.
With each loud laugh, a lesson learned,
In the deep of night.

Why chase the stars, I asked aloud,
When they just wink and run?
Perhaps I'll aim for toast instead,
At least it's warm and fun!

In search of meaning's tangled web,
I found a bubble tea.
Each sip a giggle, each slurp a clue,
My purpose, frothy glee.

Was it wisdom, or was it fruit?
The riddle makes me grin.
To seek is merry, to find is sweet,
With laughter, we begin.

## Delights and Dilemmas in the Pursuit of Truth

I sought the truth in breakfast beans,
But found it in some pie.
Balancing toast with hopes anew,
As butterflies did fly.

With questions that bounced like bouncy balls,
I lost them in a dream.
Truth wore a silly clownish nose,
It giggled, "What a scheme!"

In the garden of ponderous thoughts,
A flower petal spoke.
"Follow me to the land of smiles,
Where wisdom plays a joke!"

Thus I danced in the fields of blue,
With wisdom's candy cane.
Seeking truth was quite a ride,
With joy within the rain.

# The Silly Riddle of Existence

Existence came with silly strings,
Tangled in a knot.
I flipped it over, turned around,
And lost the pot I sought.

With riddles carved from birthday cake,
I tried to take a bite.
But sprinkles fell and laughter rose,
In sheer, delightful plight.

A penguin offered me a hat,
It said, "Let's take a ride."
We slid down paths of giggling dreams,
Where thoughts can safely glide.

In the silly riddle's dance,
I found my heart's delight.
Existence, wrapped in funny sounds,
Became my guiding light.

## Jester's Journey Through the Absurd

In a world where clowns take flight,
Bananas peel under the moonlight.
Searching for sense in jumbled thoughts,
My mind's a circus, and I'm the boss!

With floppy shoes and a squeaky horn,
I wander paths both silly and worn.
Every sign points to jest and glee,
What's serious here? Oh, let it be!

I tripped on wisdom, fell on my face,
Laughter echoes in this madcap race.
A sage's riddle? I've lost the plot,
Yet every giggle is a lesson taught!

In tangled tales, I find delight,
Chasing rainbows that burst in flight.
The more I search, the more I see,
Absurdly lovely chaos is key!

## Chasing Shadows in a Silly Serenade

With a kazoo and a bright umbrella,
I waltz with ghosts and dance with fella.
Shadows whisper in rhymes so wild,
Mischief managed like a playful child.

Bouncing from laughter to stunned surprise,
The world is upside down, just look at the skies!
Smiling clouds throw pies with glee,
Wit and whimsy are all I see!

Juggling fears like vibrant balls,
I tumble down with gleeful calls.
Notes of a tune that tickles the ear,
What once was lost is now right here!

And when the shadows twist and sway,
I'll join their dance, come what may.
For in this serenade of silly song,
I find my heart, where I belong!

## The Great Giggle Quest of an Unraveled Mind

Oh, what a quest, my mind's askew,
In search of laughter, bright and new.
Maps are scribbles, directions wrong,
But jokes are treasures, and I am strong!

Through valleys deep of chuckles and tears,
I ride a unicycle, facing my fears.
The land of absurd, where nonsense reigns,
In every pun, I loosen my chains.

Search high and low, the whoopee cushions,
For wisdom found in silly musings.
Each giggle unlocked is a door to roam,
In this folly, I finally feel home!

So twist and twirl in the inane glow,
I celebrate each laugh, let it flow.
Unraveled and free, with comedy blazed,
My heart sings loud in this joyful maze!

## Amidst the Chaos, a Chuckle

In the whirl of life with its dizzying spin,
I find my truth where the mayhem begins.
Like a cat in a hat chasing its tail,
Silly and lost, yet I shall prevail!

With socks on my hands, I declare a jest,
Each goof and blunder is an honored guest.
I tiptoe through puddles of jelly and cream,
In chaos, I thrive, a surreal dream!

Laughter erupts like popcorn in haste,
Nothing is serious, what a fun taste!
The world can be mad, yet I choose to see,
The cosmic joke played just for me!

So here's to the chaos, the laughter we share,
In the absurdity, I breathe the fresh air.
With a chuckle and wink, I carry my grin,
In this wild, funny ride, let the fun begin!

## The Lost Laughter of a Dreamer

In a land where dreams take flight,
I tripped over my own delight.
With a map drawn in crayon, oh what a sight,
I chased silly clouds through the day and night.

A jester's hat perched on my head,
I danced with squirrels, all out of spread.
Each giggle was gold, the best kind of thread,
Until I realized my shoe was a bed.

With laughter like bubbles, I puffed and I pouted,
Every punchline delivered, though none had been doubted.
The punchline's a rabbit, the joke is a crowded,
I laughed 'til I cried, feeling quite clouded.

But the wisdom of whimsy was lost in the fun,
I sought something meaningful, but found my undone.
A treasure of laughter, in jokes we had spun,
I searched for deep answers, but missed out on sun.

## Searching for Sense in Nonsense

I sat with a chicken to solve life's big riddle,
She clucked out some wisdom while playing a fiddle.
A three-legged dog played the role of dribbler,
And I scribbled my thoughts, feeling quite another middle.

How do fish share secrets in watery dreams?
While penguins provide ice with their wild themes.
I ponder the signals, or so it seems,
Yet all I have is a sandwich and cream.

Through the funhouse mirrors of life's fleeting jest,
I painted my worries, laid them to rest.
With the laughter of chaos, I laughed with the best,
In nonsense I linger, finding my quest.

But while searching for sense, I laughed way too hard,
Each giggle a compass, all life's hazards charred.
A carnival of thoughts, at every night's guard,
Nonsense flows freely, making my heart starred.

## The Follies of Seeking Significance

I launched my balloon, seeking meaning aloft,
But it drifted away, carrying dreams soft.
With each wobble it made, my purpose was scoffed,
I giggled and wondered, was significance doffed?

I tried to be serious, wore a big frown,
But ended up tripping, fell flat on the ground.
A clown in the crowd, now look what I found,
That joy has a way of turning hearts round.

With a pie in the face, I learned life at risk,
Slipping on wisdom, ah isn't it brisk?
The meaning was laughter, wrapped in a frisk,
Every folly I stumbled into was a whisk.

Life's not a puzzle to work piece by piece,
Instead, it's a joke, packed with humor's lease.
In the search for significance, just let it cease,
And laugh till you drop; that's your sweet release.

# The Comedic Chronicles of a Wayward Heart

Once lost on a road with no signs to show,
I turned left at giggles, right at the glow.
A map made of laughter, where silliness grows,
Every twist, every turn, unknown seeds to sow.

The moon winked at me, a cheerful guide,
While squirrels played chess, all puffed up with pride.
I slipped on a banana, no reason to hide,
As my heart burst with joy on this comic ride.

With a jester's grin, I penned my wild tale,
A journey of chuckles, where dreams set sail.
The path was absurd, but I wouldn't curtail,
For a heart that's wayward, it's laughter to avail.

So let the heart wander, let it roam wild,
In the comedy of life, be forever a child.
With each giggle and snort, fresh joy is compiled,
In the chronicles of laughter, we find our mild.

## The Comedic Compass of Confusion

Woke up today, what's the plan?
Should I be a beast or a suave man?
Lost in the map of my own head,
Follow the bread crumbs, but forget the bread.

Options are plenty, they twist and spin,
Should I dance like a fool, or wear a grin?
Tried to find North, but I went south,
Spoke too soon, with a silly mouth.

Friends say, 'Just follow your heart!'
But mine's a circus, pulling apart.
The compass spins with a dizzying flair,
Lost in the woods, just me and a chair.

Laughter erupts in the mess of my quest,
Each goofy blunder has me quite blessed.
In the search for a point, oh what a ride,
With a chuckle, at least, I take it in stride.

## Amusing Antics of an Existential Explorer

I set out with zeal, thinking I'm wise,
But the map's upside down, what a surprise!
Each step I take leads to another joke,
Like stepping on gum or tripping on smoke.

I asked for direction, they pointed and laughed,
Is life one big riddle, or is it a craft?
Chasing a vision, but caught in the fray,
Finding delight in my silly ballet.

The universe winks, as chaos ensues,
I spin like a top in a pair of clown shoes.
With every misstep, the sunshine breaks through,
Existence is funny, with giggles anew.

So here I am, juggling dreams and despair,
Creating a circus out of thin air.
In the quest for a meaning, who needs a map?
Just grab a big smile, and take a short nap!

## Humor in the Haze of Life's Journey

Lost in a fog, but I've got a game,
A tickle of laughter, and none feel the same.
Each twist and turn, a combo of fate,
Like falling for puns or a two-for-one date.

With friends by my side, we trip over laughter,
Each stumble reveals a wild chapter.
A detour to nowhere, we roll with delight,
Searching for lessons in the moonlight.

In the haze of confusion, I wear my best hat,
A jester with wisdom, imagine that!
With puns on my lips and joy in my heart,
This journey's a play, and I'm just the part.

So let's raise our cups to the absurdity sweet,
With giggles and grins, it's a comical feat.
For in the thick fog where we often roam,
We find the brightest laughs lead us back home.

## The Silly Search for Solid Ground

Stumbling around, searching for truth,
But each revelation's just kiddie sleuth.
The ground keeps shifting under my feet,
Is this the right zone, or just a retreat?

I wear mismatched socks for a bold fashion claim,
In the search for meaning, who's keeping score of the game?
Keep running in circles, but look how I shine,
Finding fun in the chaos with friends and some wine.

So I dance on my toes, then I trip on a shoe,
Life's just a party if you make it so too.
In the land of confusion, we giggle and glide,
The silly search leads to joy, not to hide.

With laughter our language, we build silly rules,
Searching for wisdom, oh how we are fools!
But through all the mess, one thing is profound,
In the midst of the folly, we discover solid ground.

www.ingramcontent.com/pod-product-compliance
Lightning Source LLC
Chambersburg PA
CBHW071843160426
43209CB00003B/394